TYDE

TYDE

GUILHERME SILVINO CAPELLE

Contents

Chapter I

Low Tyde

Life is an ocean with changing tides
Emotions are waves
Some can be rogue.

Searching Alone

I am always searching for answers
Tired of lies
Looking at the stars
Hoping they'll open my eyes

Sitting on the sand
Staring at the sea
Looking for someone
Trying to find me

Insomnia

I know you are tired
I know it's late
You wanna sleep
I'm keeping you awake

I have been staring at my feet
For hours
My thoughts take me to another
Reality

Somewhere you'll want me
Somewhere you'll kiss me
You'll love me

And I will love you too

To A Bad Replier

I wish you knew the feeling
I wish I could explain in way you would understand it
So picture this:

I am lying on my side
On my bed
In my room
At night or noon
Getting anxious
Wishing you reply soon

Time is passing
I keep checking my phone and nothing's there
I can't concentrate on anything else
My thoughts are racing
But they are not taking me anywhere

Cause even if they did
My mind would place you there

It's late now
I'm still awake and fighting

Fighting against me
A fight that is far from being fair

I messaged hours ago
Until you reply, I'll keep on seeing your name
Wherever I go

So the questions start to arise
What is she doing that she can't stop a second to reply?
Where is she at?
Is she with another guy?

So that's it
I am done
Ready to give everything up
I hate her now
Fuck this, at least I tried

Oh! Hold on... Nah it's all good! She just replied.

Now you know how I feel.

Find Yourself

To find yourself you must lose yourself countless times
You must break every single inch of your heart
Cry every remaining tears
Bleed the feelings you didn't leave behind
Scream loud enough to silence the negative thoughts
Sometimes you will need to lose the hope you carry inside

Let the fire burn
Hot, high and out of control
So that it can burn all the bad memories with it
Allow time so that all of this can happen

Only then you will be healed
Only then you will be ready to feel something again
Only then you will be strong enough to be happy
Only then you will find yourself.

A Funny Situation

We got ourselves in a funny situation
Where feelings can't be expressed
Words can't be said
And affection can't be shown

We must hide our emotions deep
Under our not so thick skin
Because emotions talk too loud
And we can't deal with the noise

We must convince the brain not to think
The eyes not to see
And the mouth
Not to talk about it

Despite trying hard
We cannot convince the heart not to feel it
Or the body to not crave it
Or the lungs to breathe normally when we get closer

But the closer we get
The harder it is to convince the teeth not to bite the lips
The hand not to fix the hair
Impossible to command your eyes not to stare

It's funny
Cause within every hug
A thousand feelings are expressed
A forehead kiss says more than any existing word

Our kiss brings every feeling to the surface of our being
But we will never know
Because we kiss with our eyes closed

It's funny
It's just how it goes.

If I could say

All the things I have to say
If I could stop
My emotions from getting in the way

If before I left
You had asked me to stay
I wouldn't have gone
Too far away

I Wish there was a way
To have you back
You complete me
Cause you got everything I lack

And just like that
In a poem or two
I realise it is easier than I thought
To say... "I really miss you".

New year's poem

Another year
Another run
Last year was one hell of one

Time to look back and reflect
Upon all the shit we've done

Did you find what you were looking for?
Did you lose someone?

I know you fell down but
Did you climb back up?

How many times or things have you given up?
How many smiles did you buy?
Did you achieve your goal?

Another year is gone
But how old is your soul?
Were there feelings you decided to let go?
Are there feelings you wanna let grow?

Any feelings you had to deny?
Did you improve?
Do you ever get scared that we are running out of time?

Another year and another opportunity

So here's to the years that have gone

Here's to the pain we can let go now
Here's to the years that are yet to come
Here's to all the walls you've put down.

2004-2012

Some people only cry when feeling low
Others only look up after falling down
A lot complain about everything
Very few contemplate what's around

Always about what "I want in the future"
Rarely about "thanks for what I have now"

It's not about the big house you live in
Or the nice car you drive
All the money you have
You'll leave all that shit behind

Same way we came
Same way we die
Memories about us
are the only things that stay alive

Like when we were kids
Playing by the water
When the time didn't matter
When there was nothing better
To do than kick a ball around

We just couldn't wait
To get our bare feet on the ground
When an ice cream cone
Could turn a bad day around

We were innocent
And cared deeply about each other
Back to when boys and girls
Would hate one another

When school subjects were the hardest things we needed to
understand
When the only castle we needed to build was made of sand
If the waves destroyed it
We would laugh and build it again

Back to when
Money wouldn't buy smiles
They were for free

We grew up
But we did it so fast
I miss dreaming high like when we were kids
When I had a brand new heart
And I wasn't afraid of playing with it

When I think about how fast life is going
I feel like I'd rather go slow
Be like the kids from Neverland
And never grow

Admire the ride
The flowers along the way
The bees and taste the honey

Dream about the mountain top

But also enjoy the journey

Lucky I Read This Before It Was Too Late

"I woke up
No one by my side
Stayed up late
Didn't sleep all night

Too scared leave
Too scared to stay
Haunted by the things I never got to say

The weight on my shoulders feels insane
Hunting punchlines
To stay sane

Unfair expectations, lies, pressure to success, shame of fail-
ing
The pain...
It's just too much!

It doesn't matter how hard I try
Or how well I go
I'll never be good enough!

Enough to me
Enough to you
I wanna leave
Don't know where to

God take all my suffering
Give me hope instead

I've been trying so hard
To make peace
With the voices inside my head

But they are telling me
To give it all up
To put an end
"Don't open up, don't tell anyone, they wouldn't understand"

I think I've had enough
I am tired of hiding my feelings
To act tough"

The pressure of society and it's comparisons
Increase mental illness incidence and recurrence
Destroying families

We need to become aware of it
I encourage it heavily
So many ways to die
But major depression is just as deadly!

You're not alone
Hold on to someone you know

Look after your mental health
Scream from the top of your lungs
"I need help"!

If only

I spoke to you
Better than you spoke to me

If only when we're standing on the edge
I'd taken a step back

If only you had the patience
That I lack

If only I listened to understand and not reply
We wouldn't argue all the time

The place I wanna be

Is where nature is all see
The blooming of flowers
The sound of the sea

The place I wanna be
Is where birds sing loud
Sand, earth and grass are my only ground
Screams, bombs and shootings are not familiar sounds

The place I wanna be
Is where the food I eat
Grows
Beneath my feet
Where love
Is the only language I speak
Waves
Are the only things I seek

Where
Things aren't so hard to understand
Our castles are
Made of sand

It's full of trees
Nothing tastes bad
Close to the sea
No reason to be sad

Is where friends

Surround me
Genders get along happily
Safe place to raise a family

Adrenalin,
The waterfalls provide some.
Yesterday doesn't matter,
And we live like tomorrow will never come

A place where the fire
Will keep us warm
But the trees
Will never burn

We only give smiles away
People only have nice things to say
Every day
Is a good day

Hope I find it
Someday.

A Message To Love

You have the bad habit of coming and going whenever you
please
Often, leaving me behind.

I see you looking at me with different eyes
Smiling with different teeth
Hugging with different arms
Kissing with different lips
Hurting with different hands
And walking away with different feet.

I hate you for fucking with me.

Breathe

You were taking up so much space
Inside of me
I felt suffocated
At the presence of someone else

The memories of you
Were so loud
I couldn't hear
My own thoughts

Your speeches
Shaped my vocal cords
And now, I am not sure
The words I say are mine

My body
Might not be enough
For both of us
To live in

But if my lungs
Are not enough to breathe for the both of us
Like my shoulders weren't strong enough
To carry our relationship

I will gladly
Hold my breath
To keep you
Alive.

Suddenly

My mind gets flooded with
Images of you
And I cry like never before

I finally
Understood the lyrics
To that song
I always play on repeat

For the first time
It made sense

I realised
Paradise means nothing
In your absence

The Wind

Is powerful enough
To destroy houses
Take down buildings
And drag boats
Across the sea

But it's not powerful enough
To take the memories of you
Away from me.

What My Freedom Sounds Like

Friction between sand and feet
Heat on the surface of the skin
It almost burns but it pleases

Cold, refreshing ocean breeze
Salty lips
Red chicks

Sticky white sand
Ocean lined up with waves
Breaking perfectly offshore

Nature looking wild
But somehow
Gentle and welcoming

That sounds like freedom to me.

Promises

I asked her to promise me she wouldn't
Make promises she couldn't keep.

She smiled back at me, but didn't say a thing.

I realised that was a promise she couldn't keep.

Kia

One month
Four long weeks
Thirty sleepless nights
Seven hundred and twenty long hours
That's how long I waited for our first kiss
It was bliss

Three months
Twelve perfect weeks
Ninety intentionally sleepless nights
One thousand two hundred and sixty fast lived hours
That's how long it took me to realise I wanted to spend the
rest of my life
With you

To make you
My only plan
Cause I knew that a woman like you would make me more of
a man

The following days were spent
Making plans
Where to live
Where to go
Pretending we had the answers
To things we still don't know
Loving like we had cracked the code
The dreams you were selling
Were quickly sold

We were young
Making plans to grown old
And grey hair
The cliff house
The dogs
Our kids
They were all there

In the lifetime we planned together

One year
Twelve months
Fifty-two unforgettable weeks
Three hundred and sixty five fights
Eight thousand seven hundred and sixty hours spent on silly
arguments
That's how long it took for our forever to end

The eighty years we planned
In a couple months were gone
My feet tried to touch the floor
But there was none

Promises were broken
Our hopes sent up above
Now I know why they say "falling" before "in love".

Backspace secrets

I shouldn't
But I want it
I shouldn't want it
But I do

The need is strong
I'll end up
Messaging you

My friends
Tell me
Not to

My brain never listens
To me
It will ignore them
Too

The send button
Quickly becomes the only thing
Standing in between
Me and you

My overthinking mind awakens
Thoughts start to race
I write
Delete
Rephrase

My true words are kept by the backspace

"Hey" or should I say "Hello"?
"I shouldn't be messaging, I know"
"But your eyes are all I can see,
Your lips, all I can taste,
It's like you're stuck inside of me"

Once again
I delete
Rephrase
"Hey, how are you?"
That's better
Send.

Hope she'll understand
And feel the same
I have feelings I shouldn't have
That scares me
But fear has never been my enemy

My friends tell me to forget about you
Fuck them! I don't want to.

I Drag

You've been gone for months
I still take you everywhere I go

Let you be part of my conversations
Still speak your words
And fight to defend your point of view

Truth is, when I look at what's left
I'm not sure how much of it is me
And how much is still you

You're present in my happiest days
But you're the cause of the shit ones
And my newly addiction to whiskey "on the rocks"

Your absence is more noticeable
Than your presence ever was

My mind is a carriage
Dragging you around
Making sure you haunt me
Wherever I go

Despite knowing you're heavy
I keep on dragging
Cause I'm scared to let it go.

Chapter II

High Tyde

Girl,

I've seen broken eyes before,
And they look just like
Yours.

Girl,
I've seen people
Hiding their demons behind
A smile
That looks just like
Yours.

But I've seen
What a good heart
Looks like,
And it beats just like
Yours.

I've seen your enemy
Girl,
And she looks just like
You.

Minutes ago
I had to fight my fear,
Ignore my anxiety,
Swallow my pride,
To tell
You

I've heard
A good love story,
And it begins
Just like
Ours.

Tattoo

I've been numb
Since you left
And it's been months
Since I last felt something

So I decided to get a tattoo
Not because I liked the design or
The meaning of it
I just wanted the needle
To show me I can still bleed

I needed my flash to scream loud enough
To remind me
I'm still alive

The tattoo hurt really bad
It's strange how comforting
That felt

I watched my skin
Getting torn apart
Praying I would bleed out
All the memories of you

Counting on the needle
To destroy the dreams
Of what we
Could've been

Hoping the ink
Would hide all the feelings
I still have
For you

Wishing the design
Would simply disguise
My ego and pride

But it never did.

It only cost me a lot of money
And a hell lot of pain

Well
At least I know
That this wound
Will heal.

Sleep paralysis

I always freeze
When I see her face

Last night
I dreamt about her
My brain didn't realise
It was a dream
And I froze again.

When I woke up
I couldn't move
But I had a smile
On my mind
Because I'd seen her again.

I begged my brain
As I closed my eyes
To take me back
To that Caribbean
Paradise

But it was too late,
I was wide awake.

Bizarre

I find it bizarre
How someone's company
Might make you feel lonelier
Than being alone.

How some jokes
Are incredibly accurate.
And how people should
Take into consideration
Whatever comes before "just kidding",
And ignore words
Followed by a "but".

It's heart-breaking
To see couples allowing
Their bodies to sleep together
While their minds are miles apart.

I wish people understood
That "rebound" relationships
Are basically a toxic, manipulative environment,
Where one takes advantage of the other
Leading them on
Making them think
They're loved
While they're really being used
To numb the pain
That these cowards don't wanna go through

It makes me sick
To know that people
Are willing to break others
To heal themselves.

Bizarre
How brothers
Become strangers
Friends become
Enemies
Parents forsake
Their children
Lovers learn
To hate

And the only thing
We all have in common
Is that we have absolutely
No clue about what's going on.

The Hard One

When I decided to leave
We both knew
It couldn't be
It wouldn't be

We both deserve special,
For me, it ain't you
And for you, it ain't me,
Even though I wanted it to be.

I have been moving on
Since you left.
But seeing you with
Someone new
Broke me again

I hadn't felt the pain
Of losing you
In quite a while.
This was quite a refresher.

It's hard to explain how I feel
Put it this way:

"I am happy you found someone
That makes you smile.
I am sad I'm not him"

When I See You

Out of a sudden
My confidence is gone.

The overflowing vessel
Of pure certainty
Becomes empty.

My wise invulnerable heart
Turns innocent and fragile again,
Yet, it beats recklessly.

My overthinking mind
Takes control over my
Feet and shaky hands.

I walk away
With heaps to say
Disguising it all with a simple "Hey"!

The flame

Exists only in my mind.
But it burns hot enough
To keep me warm
Through the night.

Fate, Destiny or Luck

It might be fate
It might be destiny
Sometimes it's just dumb luck

To fall in love
With the right person
And to stay in love forever

To have feelings
That are reciprocated

To arrive at the right time
To want and not too need
To learn how to accept and be accepted
To stop wanting to fix things that aren't broken

It might be fate
It might be destiny
Sometimes it's just dumb luck

The road can be lonelier
Than you might think
The view at the top
Is not always as rewarding
As you expect it to be
But I reckon the journey
Is worth the risk

To be on the right road

To fall in love with the way
And to enjoy the view
It might be fate
It might be destiny
Sometimes it's just dumb luck.

Hiding from love

I've been giving love
Far too many chances to disappoint me.
And I'm tired of paying the price

I thought If I ignored love
For long enough
It would forget me
And find someone else to mess with

I've been hiding from it
In the dark
In a paradise of numbness

My heart tells me
I'm not welcome to stay
Love is blind
The darkness never mattered anyway

And against my will
It'll find me again.

Last Night

I kissed a girl
She looks a lot like you,
Physically wise.

Personality wise,
You two are a lot alike.

This means you're either not special at all
Or you're more special than I realised.

They don't wanna see you win

Your pain will
Bring them joy

Your tears
Will aid their thirst
And they will feast on
Your broken bones

Your failures
Will be their victories
And that shall be
The closest to winning they'll
Ever get

Your blood tastes good
In their mouths
Your sins make them holy
Your crimes give them the right
To judge and carry out your sentence

They'll feed on your insecurities
To look more confident
And to nourish their ego

They'll climb on top of anything
And anyone
To look down on you

Your nightmares

Are the sweet dreams
They've been dreaming of

Their mediocre mind
Settles for being better than you
As if that alone
Is already good enough

However
Don't give up
Because your light
Will blind them

Your truth
Shall out run
Their lies

The sight
Of your happiness
Will hurt their eyes

Your hope
Will cause anger
Your faith
Will break their bones
Your resilience
Will make them desperate

Every time you get back
On your feet
They'll fall

On their knees

When you succeed
They'll become your fans
And rise
To perform the standing ovation.

Please

Give me a reason
To stay
And I'll look past
All the reasons
To leave

Say that you're
Only one call away
And your phone
Shall ring

Break me into pieces
And build me up again
Shape me
Into your vessel
Like water in a cup

Pour my feelings
Until your heart is
Overflowing

Steal my heat
Till I'm stone cold

Breathe the air
From my lungs
Until my lips
Turn blue

Feed of my flesh
Drink of my blood

Dream of my broken dreams
Taste the tears in my eyes
Notice the demons inside
But don't be scared
They don't bite

Keep on taking
Till there's nothing left to take
Cause I'll keep on giving
Till there's nothing else
To give.

I'm growing up

Whatever that means
As I'm getting wiser
My goals are getting clearer

My opinions
Are not so strong anymore
And other's opinions no longer
Matter to me

I've grown to enjoy
A silent victory
And welcome compliments
Without relying on them

My self love
Outgrew my ego
So I no longer
Seek validation from
A single individual.

Remember

Yelling
Fighting
Crying
Pushing
Talking over someone
Leaving
Turning your back to someone
Breaking things
Insulting
Offending
Hurting with words
Violence.

These are NOT examples of good communication, and
Proper communication is what holds a relationship together.

Thanks to you

My heart learnt
How to say "hello" and "goodbye"
With the same frequency and less
Intensity.

Facts about love according to my own experiences

The only unconditional love you'll experience
In your life
Will come from your mother
And your dog.

Love can heal you with one hand
Yet, break you with the other.

Love can turn the bitter reality
Into something sweet and tasteful.

The absence of it can turn a
Fortunate life into something
Hard to digest.

Love and loyalty
Don't always walk
Side by side.

It arrives with no warning
Rocks up without being invited
Love doesn't knock on the door
It breaks in

Love doesn't ask for permission
Love takes whatever it wants
Whenever it wants
Love leaves whenever it wants.

Love never leaves empty handed.
More often than not, it takes more
Than it should.

Love never says goodbye forever.
We hope one day it finally decides
To stay.

I'm convinced that love is not blind
But the cupid fucking is.
Honestly, he has one job and he sucks at it!

Most marriages end in divorce.
I guess the boss in heaven would rather reallocate the blame
Call it a sin
Instead of replacing cupid with someone
Who actually knows
What the fuck they're doing.

Love is a drug
And it feels better when
Everyone around you
Is high on it

Love Is A Drug

And I've been dealing it for free
To get all my friends and family
High as fuck!

What is life?

If not what we perceive
It to be?

I wonder how much
Of the world
I live in
Is real

I wonder if everyone
Shares the same
Reality

I wonder how much
Of the creation
God left up to our
Imagination

What if
My emotions
My personality
My past experiences
My childhood
My Values
My Environment
My financial situation
Created a reality that is
Unique to me?

Perhaps my rights and wrongs,

My standards
Are only mine to live up to

Perhaps my opinions
Are not, at all, valid
Or relevant

Perhaps we are not all
On the same boat

We are all on the same ocean
But sailing in different directions

A breakup letter I didn't actually send

I see all your effort
I appreciate the walls
You've put down
To let me in.

I respect you,
I admire you,
I understand your struggles,
I'm not in love with you.

When we have sex,
We fuck,
We don't make love
And that says a lot.

When I leave your place
I leave with a smile on my face,
And that says even more

You are amazing.
Yet, I don't miss you.
I sleep better without you.
My bed feels bigger,
And I like that

When I see you
I don't get butterflies.

The butterflies are missing.

You are beautiful,
But receiving your text
Doesn't make my heartbeat
Any faster.

Breaking your heart
Makes me really sad.

I once felt
With someone else
The connection
I wish we had.

You deserve the world.
I am sorry I can't give it
To you.

An Analogy of Life and Relationships

We are not all on the same boat
We are all in the same ocean
But each on their own boat.

When we are young
Our parents will act as the wind
And be the captains of our ship
They'll power our engines
And choose in which directions we'll sail.
Usually according to their values and beliefs.

When we grow up
We become too heavy
To be pushed around
So, we must begin our own journey.

We start drifting away from our parents
Anchor,
And we must choose which currents
To follow,
Based on where we wanna go.

Given that we are all born into this massive ocean
With infinite tides, currents and destinations
We all must pick a direction to sail towards to.

Some are born with bigger and better boats
And that might make the navigation easier and comfier.
But in the end, we are all navigating the same waters,

Scared of the same waves and facing the same
Storms,
Trying to stay afloat.

People will choose different directions in life
Based on what they want out of the journey and
What they think their destination will be.

Some will change courses a couple times
Some will get somewhere
Some will die trying.

When we let someone into our life
We are letting them inside our boat
We must ensure this person has chosen
A similar route to a similar destination

Cause for a boat to move forward
Both sailors must row at the same time
In the same direction.

If you'd like to go left
And your partner right
Both can row as hard as you can
The boat would only be spinning around in circles
And neither of you would go anywhere.
You'd be stuck!

If your partner is rowing in the same direction as you
You'll navigate faster, easier and in a more enjoyable way.
However, if at some point they choose to sail

In another direction
You must ask them to leave your boat
Or it will sink when the storm arrives.

Remember: "Life is an ocean. Emotions are waves, and some can be rogue.

Acknowledgements

Poetry has been my life-saving vest. Poetry found me in 2018 when I had lost myself. Therefore, I cannot publish this book without acknowledging the vital role that Laura Ferreira played in my life. I thank you Laura for bringing out the creative and sensitive part of me.

My poetry was taken to another level after I encountered with Kia Centonze in my journey through life. She taught me how to communicate better and she was one of my biggest supporters through a period of my life. I thank you Kia for believing in me. Thus, making me believe too.

A special thank you to Matheus Ladeira, Gustavo Linardi, Victoria Bandeira, Lavínia Bandeira, Victor Marcatto, Bruno Fornari, Cicero Tavares, Mariana Nakamoto, Lily Smith, Jamie Norman and all my friends whom throughout the years have patiently listened to my poems and given me criticism on them. I know I am not always easy to deal with, but thank you for being there for me.

Finally, I cannot leave my family out of it. Thank you Rosangela Bueno, Laercio Bueno, Yule Silvino, Felipe Bueno, Clotilde Valillo, Antonio Carlos Silvino, and every single person who raised me and made me become who I am today.